Samuel Eaton's Day

A Day in the Life of a Pilgrim Boy

by KATE WATERS

Photographs by

RUSS KENDALL

SCHOLASTIC
HARDCOVER

SCHOLASTIC INC.
New York

Many thanks to the staff and volunteers at Plimoth Plantation, particularly: Liz Lodge, Vice President of Exhibits; Carolyn Freeman Travers, Director of Research; Maureen Richard, Associate Curator; Lisa Whalen, Village Supervisor; Nanepashemet, Director of the Wampanoag Indian Program; Pat Baker, Wardrobe and Textile Manager; Kathleen Curtin, Foodways Manager; Regina Scotland, Foodways Assistant; Jill Costa, Wardrobe Associate; Carol City, Director of Public Relations; Paula Fisher, Marketing and Public Relations Associate; Marie Donlan, Receptionist; Ben Emery, Videographer; Tom Wilson, Security; Marie Pelletier, Graphics.

More thanks than we can measure to the "cast": Roger Burns, who is Samuel; Martha Sulya, who is Mam; Gary Farias, who is Samuel's father; Eric Parkman, who is Robert Bartlett; Joshua Bailey, who is Rachel; Linda Coombs and Julie Roberts, who are Penashamuk and Ammapoo; Amelia Poole, who is (again) Sarah Morton; Scott Atwood, Rick Currier, Jon Lane, Matthew Pedersen, George Sampson, David Walbridge, and Lisa Walbridge, Colonial Interpreters; Trapezious the cat; and Antic the goat.

And thanks to the supporting cast: Joy and Erin Burns; Regina Scotland (again, but this time for lending Joshua to us); Stuart Bolton and Tom Gerhardt; and David Rees, the ablest and most congenial of photographer's assistants.

To Marijka Kostiw, Associate Art Director, for making the most of our words and pictures, and to Dianne Hess, our editor, for her total involvement in this book and her support while we went about it.

Photographs on pp. 36 and 39, courtesy of Plimoth Plantation. Woodcuts on p. 38 by Heather Saunders.

"The Marriage of Frogge and Mouse," p. 35 from *Melismata, Musicall Phansies*, by Thomas Ravenscroft. Originally published in London in 1611. Printed by William Stansby for Thomas Adams.

To Thomas Fitzgerald Weir, godson and adventurer.
—K.W.

To Roy Chaston, who lent me my first camera.
—R.K.

Library of Congress Cataloging-in-Publication Data

Waters, Kate.
Samuel Eaton's day: a day in the life of a pilgrim boy/
by Kate Waters; photographed by Russ Kendall.
p. cm.
Summary: Text and photographs follow a young pilgrim boy
through a busy day during the summer harvest in 1627:
doing chores, getting to know his Wampanoag Indian neighbors,
and spending time with his family.
ISBN 0-590-46311-X
1. Pilgrims (New Plymouth Colony) — Juvenile literature.
2. Massachusetts — History — New Plymouth, 1620–1691 — Juvenile literature.
[1. Pilgrims (New Plymouth Colony)
2. Massachusetts — Social life and customs — Colonial period, ca. 1600–1775.]
I. Kendall, Russ, ill. II. Title.
F68.W325   1993
974.4'8202 — dc20   92-32325
CIP
AC
12 11 10 9 8 7 6 5 4 3 2   5 6 7 8/9
Printed in the U.S.A.   36
First Scholastic printing, September 1993

Designed by Marijka Kostiw

The photographs in this book
were taken with a Nikon F4 camera
and 20 mm, 85 mm, and 180 mm Nikkor lenses.
Some scenes were lit with Norman 400B portable lights.
Mr. Kendall used Fujichrome 50 film.

July 16, 1627

Good day to you. I am Samuel Eaton. My family sailed from England to this New World seven years ago on the ship *Mayflower.*

I was a mere sucking child then and I don't remember the voyage or our first winter here. Nearly half the people died. My mother was one. Father and Mam are married now, and I have a wee sister called Rachel.

Today is the day I have been longing for. I am to help with the rye harvest for the first time. It is my beginning to be a man. If I can show Father that I am up to the task, perhaps he will let me help with all the harvest.

This is our village, Plimoth Plantation.
The land was wild when we first came ashore.
My father's talents as a carpenter have been
much in demand in this new land. He has aided
in the building of all you see.

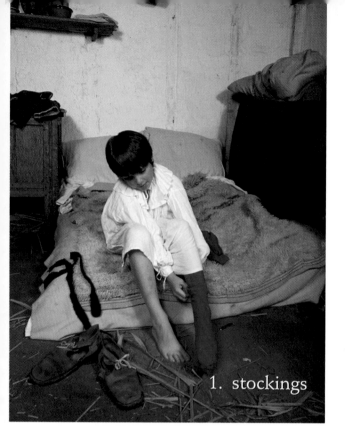

1. stockings

I am up at first light. I am so eager, I have hardly slept. I get out of bed and get dressed.

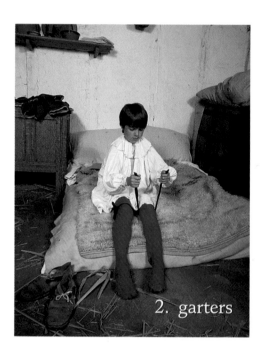

2. garters

3. breeches

4. doublet

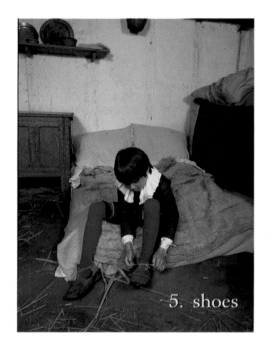

5. shoes

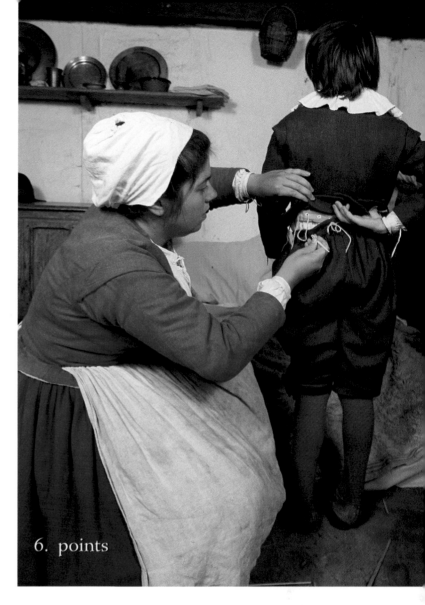

6. points

Mam helps me tie my points.

"Go then quickly now, Samuel," she says. "Thou must tend to thy labors before thou goest to the fields. And thou mustn't keep thy father waiting this morn, lest he leave thee behind."

7. hat

First, I go to the spring to fetch water. My friend Sarah Morton is out early as well. I stop for a moment, though I shouldn't. I tell her that I am glad to be aiding with the harvest and that I am afeared of being gammy at the work.

She laughs and says, "Thou art a grown boy in breeches now, Samuel, not a baby in long clothes. Thou art strong enough for the labor."

Her words send me on my way.

Now that I am almost grown, I can help catch game for the table. I run into the woods to check my snare. Father has finally let me set my own this season. It is empty this morn, but it is well placed and may soon give us a fat coney for a pottage.

I straighten the loop to set the snare again.

On the way back I gather firewood. I need to get Mam much to keep the fire while Father and I are on the rye ground.

In other seasons, Mam would go with Father to reap. Now she is not feeling well. Methinks I will have a new brother or sister!

I know that Mam will miss my help, but I'd as lief try to do a man's work this day.

Before breakfast, I brush my clothes and wash my hands and face.

Father says a blessing before we eat.

O Lord our God and heavenly Father, which of thy unspeakable mercy towards us, hast provided meate and drinke for the nourishment of our weake bodies. Grant us peace to use them reverently, as from thy hands, with thankful hearts: let thy blessing rest upon these thy good creatures, to our comfort and sustentation: and grant we humbly beseech thee good Lord, that as we doe hunger and thirst for this food of our bodies, so our soules may earnestly long after the food of eternall life, through Jesus Christ our Lord and Saviour, Amen.

I serve Father and Mam the samp.

Rachel is learning to eat upgrown food. Some goes in, but she loses somewhat by the way!

13

After breakfast, tis time to go. It seems to take Father a long time to be ready.

Tis no time to dally lest a summer storm come over. Our stores are low now, and all depends on getting the harvest in. We will have naught to eat this winter if we are slack and let the birds or the rains spoil the grain.

Finally we set out. Our neighbor Robert Bartlett is to help us with the harvest. He is not yet wed and has but one acre of his own. Father will share our grain in return for his labor.

As we pass through the village gate, Father tells me about his first rye harvest.

Our ground seems so vast. Since first planting, my friends and I have come out here to scare the birds and coneys away from the new plants.

Most of our ground is planted with Indian corn, and some with barley. But that will not be ready for reaping until later. The rye is ready now. Robert Bartlett says it will take but a few days to harvest the rye.

I am not grown enough to wield the sickle. It can cut a man's arm so I stay a distance behind. Father and Robert Bartlett reap the rye with the sickle and lay it behind. It is my task to gather and bind the rye.

Robert Bartlett shows me how to bind. At first I am
gammy and fall behind. To watch is easy. To do is hard.
The straw is coarse and makes my hands smart
and my skin itch, if truth be told. And the sun burns
my neck. But I'll say narry a word. Tis but folly to
spend time in bootless complaints.

Father and Robert Bartlett sing while they cut:

It was the frog in the well, humble dum humble dum;
And the merry mouse in the mill, tweedle tweedle twino.

Tis a song with many verses and helps pass the time.
I try to join in but I am truly thinking of my empty
stomach and sore hands. Perhaps I was foolish to think
I could do a man's work!

When the sun is high I finally see Mam and Rachel coming with dinner. Of a sudden I feel small and tis a struggle not to weep. But I mustn't let Father see.

We sit under a shady tree and have bread and cheese and cold water from the spring. My legs and back ache. I am surely grateful to rest!

When Mam notices my blisters, she takes me to the brook to cool my hands.

"They will harden thy hands like a man's hands soon," she says. Mam is quiet for a time. Then she says, "Art thou faring well, Samuel? Be thou too done to remain?"

I tell her that I must remain, that I want to help bring in the rye though I truly am done. I am grateful that Mam does not fret overly and I think she will not tell Father how much I smart.

I lay down to rest by the brook.
Tis a place I could stay till morning!

Of a sudden Father is calling. He
shows me how to hone the sickle.
Then it is time to go back to the rye.

We reap and bind until the sun is setting. I have straw in my breeches and down my neck and itch all over.

My way with the rye seems harder now, not easier. But I do not fall so far behind.

At last the sun is setting.

On the way home Robert Bartlett and I stop to gather mussels for the evening meal. They are slippery and cling to the rocks, and the salt water stings my hands.

Penashamuk and Ammapoo are gathering as well. We say good evening and turn towards home.

I lag behind. Then Robert Bartlett calls to me. He tells me I worked better today than ever he did at my age. He says he hopes someday to have a son as strong as I.

I am truly pleased and stand a bit taller.

It is nearly dark when we get home. Though I am more weary than I remember, I blow bubbles with Rachel and set her to sleep. She will always want to get in Mam's way.

Mam chops the parsley to flavor the mussels.

We eat our fill of mussels and curds.
Mam asks me about the rest of the day.

There will be no schooling for me tonight because Father has the watch. He puts on his armor, bandolier, and powder flask. I hold his musket. Of a sudden, Father asks for a word with me.

At the gate, I am quiet though I long to ask how I fared. We smell the air for rain and listen for the cries of wolves who want our cattle.

"Thou wert a fine help this day, son. Dost think thou canst keep at the harvest with the upgrown people?" Father asks.

"Oh, surely!" I say, and of a sudden the blisters and aches aren't important.

I watch as Father walks up the hill to the fort and wonder at his strength. My legs will barely take me to the house.

I undress and fall into bed. Rachel wakes up
and wants to play. I quiet her with one of the
songs we sang today.

It was the frog in the well, humble dum humble dum;
And the merry mouse in the mill, tweedle tweedle twino.

Though my hands tingle and my legs are stiff, tis a man's hurts I am feeling. I pray that I will be able to keep up to Father's faith in me, that the rains won't come before the harvest is done, that my snare will catch a fat coney for Mam, and that God will protect us.

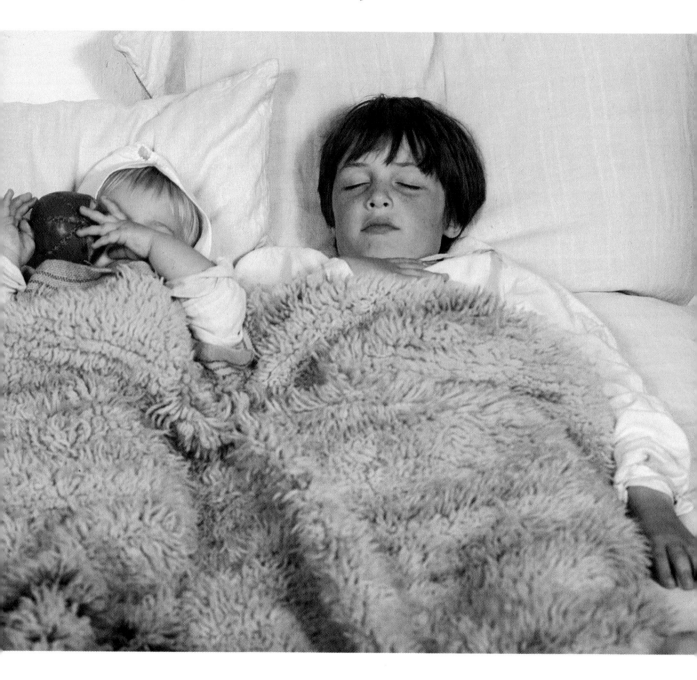

Fare thee well with thy labors.
God keep thee.

The Marriage of the Frogge and the Movse.

Treble. **21.** **4. Voc.**

T'was the Frogge in the well, Humble-dum, humble-dum. And the merrie Mouse in the Mill, tweedle, tweedle twino.

It was the frog in the well, humble dum humble dum;
And the merry mouse in the mill, tweedle tweedle twino.

The frog would a wooing ride, humble dum humble dum;
Sword and buckler by his side, tweedle tweedle twino.

When he was upon his high horse set, humble dum humble dum;
His boots they shone as black as soot, tweedle tweedle twino.

When she came to the merry millpin, humble dum humble dum;
Lady Mouse been you within? tweedle tweedle twino.

Then came out the dusty mouse, humble dum humble dum;
I am the Lady of this house, tweedle tweedle twino.

Hast thou any mind of me? humble dum humble dum;
I have e'ne great mind of thee, tweedle tweedle twino.

Who shall this marriage make? humble dum humble dum;
Our lord which is the rat, tweedle tweedle twino.

What shall we have to our supper? humble dum humble dum;
Three beans in a pound of butter, tweedle tweedle twino.

When supper they were at, humble dum humble dum;
The frog, the mouse, and even the rat, tweedle tweedle twino.

Then came in Gib our cat, humble dum humble dum;
And catched the mouse even by the back, tweedle tweedle twino.

Then did they separate, humble dum humble dum;
And the frog lept on the floor so flat, tweedle tweedle twino.

Then came in Dick our drake, humble dum humble dum;
And drew the frog even to the lake, tweedle tweedle twino.

The rat run up the wall, humble dum humble dum;
A goodly company, the devil go with all, tweedle tweedle twino.

About Plimoth Plantation

Plimoth Plantation is the outdoor living history museum of seventeenth-century Plymouth, Massachusetts. The museum portrays life as it was led by the English colonists who came to Plymouth in 1620, and by their Wampanoag neighbors. Visitors may explore *Mayflower II*, a full-scale reproduction of the type of ship that brought the Pilgrims to the New World; Hobbamock's (Wampanoag Indian) Homesite, a re-creation of the lifestyle and customs of the Native People of that region; and the 1627 Pilgrim Village.

At the Plantation's Pilgrim Village, the year is always 1627. Almost seven years have passed since the first settlers left the chaos of Europe behind in order to establish their own church and to gain economic prosperity.

The modern visitor may converse with the interpreters as they go about their daily chores, which vary by the season. Each interpreter has taken the role of a real-life 1627 Plymouth resident in dress, dialect, and religious philosophy.

Within the walls of the palisade, rough-hewn and clapboard houses, each with its own kitchen garden, are set alongside an earthen street that gently slopes downhill to the Atlantic Ocean. Sheep, goats, and cattle graze contentedly; chickens, roosters, and cats wander in and out of houses; and the smell of baking bread and bubbling fish stew wafts through the air.

Time is suspended as Plimoth Plantation keeps our early American heritage vibrantly alive.

Mayflower II

Notes About the Book

Who Was Samuel Eaton?

Samuel Eaton was seven years old in 1627. He and his family sailed to the New World on the *Mayflower*, the first English ship to bring colonists to Plymouth, Massachusetts. The Eaton family came to the New World for economic reasons, not for religious ones. They were probably originally from Bristol, England.

The *Mayflower* landed first on Cape Cod, but the travelers didn't find a suitable place for a settlement so they continued to Plymouth. Because it was winter and the Pilgrims had to build houses to live in, many spent most of the winter living on board the ship. More than half of the passengers, including Samuel's mother, died that first winter of overexposure to the cold, and inadequate diet.

Samuel's father, Francis, was a carpenter. He traded his skill for goods, and the family was neither the poorest nor the richest in the village. Samuel's father remarried, and Rachel was born. In the years after 1627, Samuel's stepmother had two more children.

Samuel grew up and apprenticed for seven years in husbandry, which is farming. Then he married and had his own farm, first in Duxbury and then in Middleboro, Massachusetts. Samuel married twice and had six children. The four about whom there are records were named Sarah, Samuel, Mercy, and Bethiah. Samuel lived to be 64 years old.

Meet Roger Burns

Roger Burns was seven years old in the summer of 1992 when these photographs were taken. He was about to begin second grade. Both of Roger's parents are descendents of *Mayflower* passengers. And they still live in Plymouth! Roger's mother is an interpreter at Plimoth Plantation, so although Roger does not yet work at the Plantation, he is familiar with the village and many of the staff.

Looking back on the week of taking pictures, Roger remembers that the clothes were very hot and the water pail was very heavy. He particularly enjoyed being photographed with the baby. Roger would sing songs and make noises to keep the baby entertained. He also liked the lunch shot because, for the first time, he discovered that he likes Dutch cheese!

Roger hasn't decided what he wants to be when he gets older, but he says that he has learned a lot about patience from working on this book. During the long waits while the photographer set up the lights and the museum staff checked the setting, Roger played electronic games, learned how to make a blade of grass whistle between his thumbs, and rounded up hens and roosters.

Sowing

Reaping

Binding

About the Rye Harvest

The Plimoth Plantation settlers brought many seeds with them from England. They did not really know where they would settle, and so they didn't know what kinds of plants they would find. In 1627, the villagers were growing Indian corn, which was a native plant, and barley, wheat, and rye from seeds originally carried from England. They used Indian corn to make flour, and traded it among themselves for other food or services, such as blacksmithing and carpentry. They also traded corn for fur with the Native People to send back to England to pay taxes to the English investors who put up the money for their voyage. They used barley to make beer, and wheat and rye to make flour for bread, pancakes, and pastries.

Rye seeds were usually planted in September, although occasionally they were planted in early spring. When the rye was ripe, it was cut and bound in sheaves. The sheaves were stacked together in shocks and left in the field to dry. Then the men threshed the rye. They beat the stalks so that the tiny grains fell out. Next the women winnowed the grain outdoors to remove the thin covering around the grain. (The covering is like the skin around some peanuts.) They put some grain in a wide, shallow basket. Then they tossed the grain up in the air. The grain kernels fell back into the basket, and the coatings blew away in the wind.

Women and children then ground the grains into flour using a mortar and pestle. Usually people made only as much flour as they needed, and kept the grain stored in barrels or sacks. The straw that was left behind from the threshing was used to thatch roofs, to stuff mattresses, and as bedding for their animals.

Threshing

Winnowing

Grinding

Of Long Clothes and Breeches

In the seventeenth century, both boys and girls wore dresses until they were six or seven years old. Dresses for very young children had strings attached to the backs of them, called leading strings (*see page 20*), so that a parent or an older brother or sister could keep the child from falling down while he or she was learning to walk. When a boy was about seven years old, he got his first pair of breeches. Boys looked forward to wearing breeches because it meant that they were almost grown.

The Wampanoag People

Wampanoag means "Eastern people." The Wampanoag and other Native Peoples shared the land we now call Massachusetts. They hunted and fished and farmed. The Native Peoples had been trading furs with European traders for years before the *Mayflower* landed. But the *Mayflower* brought the first group of European people who would settle permanently on Wampanoag land.

The women Samuel greets in this book are wearing a combination of Wampanoag and English clothes (*see page 26*). They got the English clothes either as gifts or by trading. The red blanket was worn like a shawl for warmth.

Glossary

Bandolier — a strap worn across the chest to carry vials of gunpowder.................... 30

Bind — to tie 16

Bootless — groundless, useless... 18

Breeches — knee-length pants ... 6

Coney — adult rabbit 9

Curds — a soft cheese that hasn't been pressed or aged, such as cottage cheese 29

Dally — waste time, dawdle..... 14

Done — tired out 22

Doublet — jacket................ 6

Fetch — get 8

Folly — foolish 18

Gammy — clumsy............... 8

Garters — bands used to hold up stockings 6

Ground — fields 10

Hone — sharpen 23

Lest — in case 7

Lief — rather 10

Long clothes — long, dresslike clothes worn by young boys and girls until they were five or six years old.............. 8

Morn — morning............... 7

Mussels — edible shellfish 26

Narry — not 18

Naught — nothing.............. 14

Points — strings used to lace doublet and breeches together.. 7

Pottage — thick stew........... 9

Reap — cut 10

Rye — a cereal grass whose seeds are used to make flour .. 3

Samp — cracked corn cooked to a mush 13

Sickle — a tool with a curved blade used to cut grain stalks... 16

Slack — lazy or forgetful 14

Smart — hurt 22

Snare — a rope trap for catching animals 9

Spring — a pool of fresh water that comes from the earth 8

Stockings — long socks 6

Stores — supplies of food 14

Straw — stalks seeds grow on... 18

Sucking child — nursing infant .. 3

Upgrown — grown-up........... 13

Watch — guard duty 30

Weary — tired 29

Wee — little or young........... 3

Wield — use 16